True Life

Alice Paul

VOTES FOR WOM

VOTES FOR WOMEN

Dona Herweck Rice

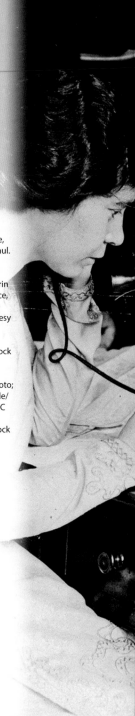

Consultants

Timothy Rasinski, Ph.D.
Kent State University

Lori Oczkus, M.A.
Literacy Consultant

Publishing Credits

Rachelle Cracchiolo, M.S.Ed., *Publisher*
Conni Medina, M.A.Ed., *Managing Editor*
Dona Herweck Rice, *Series Developer*
Emily R. Smith, M.A.Ed., *Content Director*
Stephanie Bernard/Noelle Cristea, M.A.Ed., *Editors*
Robin Erickson, *Senior Graphic Designer*

The TIME logo is a registered trademark of TIME Inc. Used under license.

Image Credits: Cover and p. 1 (foreground) LOC [LC-DIG-hec-06766], (background) Universal History Archive/Getty Images; Reader's Guide page, pp.7–10 Photographs courtesy of the Alice Paul Institute, Inc., www.alicepaul. org; p.2 LOC [mnwp.155018]; p.5 Peter Stackpole/Life Magazine/The LIFE Picture Collection/Getty Images; p.6 Robert M. Hunt Wikimedia Commons License: Creative Commons BY-SA 3.0/ https://goo.gl/m4aBf8; pp.10-11 Sarin Images/Granger, NYC; p.12 Gianni Dagli Orti/The Art Archive at Art Resource, NY; p.13 The Print Collector/Print Collector/Getty Images; pp.14-15, 23 (bottom) Granger, NYC; p.16 507 collection/Alamy Stock Photo; p.18 Courtesy Friends Historical Library of Swarthmore College; p.19 Photo by MPI/Getty Images; p.20 age fotostock/Alamy Stock Photo; p.21 Universal History Archive/UIG via Getty Images; pp.22, 29, 43 Everett Collection IncAlamy Stock Photo; p.23 (top) Kean Collection/Getty Images; pp.26, 28 Heritage Image Partnership Ltd/Alamy Stock Photo; p.31 LOC [LC-USZC4-6471]; p.32 PF-(bygone1)/Alamy Stock Photo; p.33 World History Archive/Alamy Stock Photo; p.34 American Photo Archive/Alamy Stock Photo; p.35, back page Chronicle/Alamy Stock Photo; p.36 Harris & Ewing/Buyenlarge/Getty Images; p.38 LOC Prints and Photographs: Suffragette Movement, USA; p.40 World History Archive/Alamy Stock Photo; all other images from iStock and/or Shutterstock

Library of Congress Cataloging-in-Publication Data

Names: Rice, Dona, author.
Title: True life, Alice Paul / Dona Herweck Rice ; consultants, Timothy Rasinski, Ph.D., Kent State University Lori Oczkus, M.A.
Description: Huntington Beach : Teacher Created Materials, 2017. | Includes index.
Identifiers: LCCN 2016052110 (print) | LCCN 2016059185 (ebook) | ISBN 9781493836352 (pbk.) | ISBN 9781480757394 (eBook)
Subjects: LCSH: Paul, Alice, 1885-1977. | Suffragists--United States--Biography. | Women--Suffrage--United States--History. | Women's rights--United States--History.
Classification: LCC HQ1413.P38 R53 2017 (print) | LCC HQ1413.P38 (ebook) | DDC 324.6/23092 [B] --dc23
LC record available at https://lccn.loc.gov/2016052110

Teacher Created Materials

5301 Oceanus Drive
Huntington Beach, CA 92649-1030
http://www.tcmpub.com

ISBN 978-1-4938-3635-2

Table of Contents

Conviction

Purpose. Assurance. **Conviction** . . . at all costs.

Where does a person find the fortitude and passion to put everything on the line, including her life, to right society's wrongs? How does she persist when public opinion and, more importantly, those in power actively and violently oppose her? How does she take a stand knowing she may be harassed, tortured, and even potentially killed? And knowing this, how does she find the will and the **tenacity** to persevere regardless of the outcome?

Hand to the Plow

"When you put your hand to the plow, you can't put it down until you get to the end of the row." That is what Paul had to say when asked why she lived her life dedicated to women's **suffrage**.

She does what she does simply because she must. She knows only one truth, and that is the clarity of her conviction. It is worth everything—*everything*—to stand up and be heard. Her inner guidance is so clear that choice is all but removed from her experience. To breathe is to force action. She charges forward, **undaunted** and **resolute**.

Stand, speak, fight—she ignites a revolution in the name of women's rights. And history is finally, irrevocably set on a new path.

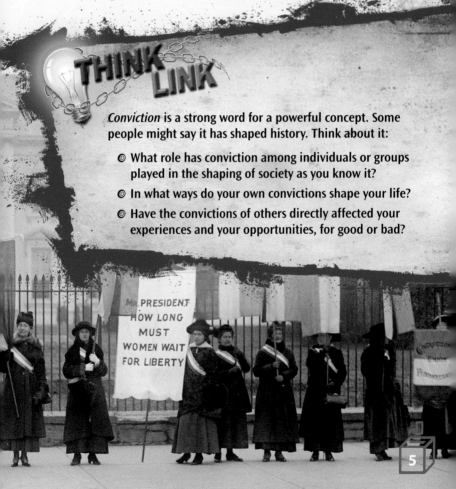

THINK LINK

Conviction is a strong word for a powerful concept. Some people might say it has shaped history. Think about it:

- ◎ What role has conviction among individuals or groups played in the shaping of society as you know it?
- ◎ In what ways do your own convictions shape your life?
- ◎ Have the convictions of others directly affected your experiences and your opportunities, for good or bad?

Mr. PRESIDENT HOW LONG MUST WOMEN WAIT FOR LIBERTY

Paulsdale

Experts agree that the first few years of life are **crucial** in shaping who a person becomes. About the age that most children begin kindergarten, the human brain has shaped and molded much of who that person is and what that person knows and does. Behaviors, character traits, and life purpose all take their shapes. If this is true, then the mind and heart of Alice Paul can be found in Paulsdale, her family's home.

Alice Stokes Paul was born on January 11, 1885. Chester Arthur was president, the Statue of Liberty was on its way to New York Harbor, and the first of William and Tacie Paul's four children was about to make her way into the world. The baby was born at the family's "home farm," as Paul called it, in Mount Laurel, New Jersey, arriving healthy, strong, and ready to meet the world head-on.

And that's just what she did.

Paulsdale, the family home

Preservation

Paul's family home and acres of land have been preserved as a National Historic Landmark. At this book's printing, Paulsdale is among the few U.S. historic landmarks—under four percent—that are dedicated to the memories and legacies of women.

Alice as a baby with her mother, Tacie

Tacie Paul and the Suffragists

Paul's mother, Tacie, was a firm believer in equal rights. Tacie was a member of the National American Woman Suffrage Association (NAWSA). Suffragists sought the right for women to vote. They frequently included the rights of nonwhites in their efforts, since at that time only white men could vote. When the Fifteenth Amendment to the U.S. Constitution was passed, women were left out. NAWSA worked to change that.

Paul was born into comfort and ease, since her family did very well in the world. Her father, William, was president of a trust company in Moorestown, New Jersey. Although Paulsdale was a roughly 200-acre working farm, the family had the **means** to hire laborers to run it. Paul and her siblings didn't need to work strenuously on the farm, as many farm children of the time did, although they did have chores and responsibilities. Even so, they had time and space to explore and create. Their parents believed strongly in the need for all people—especially children—to stay close to nature and to live connected to the natural world. Because of these roots, Paul had an active and happy childhood.

Alice (age 6) and her brother Billy (age 4)

Athlete

As a child, Alice loved sports and played baseball, basketball, and field hockey.

Alice Paul Institute

Today, Paulsdale not only stands as a National Historic Landmark but also serves as the home of the Alice Paul Institute, an organization that carries on the legacy of Alice Paul by "educating and empowering women and girls from all segments of society to take leadership roles in their schools and communities."

Early Life

Paulsdale offered many comforts for the family. By the turn of the century, the house had electricity and indoor plumbing. Although the family chose to live simply in many ways, they still enjoyed such modern pleasures as a telephone and a tennis court!

Paul could often be found reading on the huge porch that wrapped around the family home. Her love of learning and quick intellect made her an outstanding student. She did quite well in her classes at a Moorestown school. At a time when few women pursued college, Paul's future in the academic world was practically decided. It was part of the family's religious **ideology** as members of the Religious Society of **Friends** that women be treated as equals. The Friends, more commonly known as **Quakers**, were at the foundation of not only Paulsdale but also Alice Paul herself. Paul's abilities and her family's belief in the equality of women had made college an obvious choice.

First in Class

When Paul graduated from high school in 1901, she was just 16 years old and the top student in her school.

The red and black Quaker Service Star is a symbol of service and compassion.

Quakers

The Religious Society of Friends began in England in the mid-1600s as part of widespread religious reform. This Christian religion did away with nearly all traditional church practices, such as sacraments and **clergy**. Every Friend is called to listen to his or her inner guidance and share that guidance with others. Quaker gatherings of Paul's time would involve Friends sitting together in silence until one felt compelled by God to speak. The influence of Quakers on Paul's life cannot be overstated.

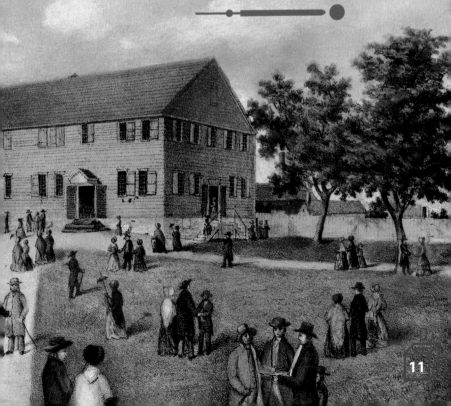

Hicksite Quakers

In the early 1800s, broad **dissent** and changes swept through the Friends movement. A large group of Quakers wished to infuse their practices and beliefs with modern reforms, while others, led by the strong-spoken Elias Hicks, wanted to keep things as they were. The group of Hicks's supporters became known as Hicksite, while those who wished to change were called Orthodox. Paul and her family were Hicksite Quakers.

There are core **fundamental** beliefs that are part of the Quaker faith and were sacred to Alice Paul. Quakers believe in the equality of the genders and all races. They also believe in **pacifism**, education for all, and the need to work to correct society's faults.

Hicksite Quakers strongly affirm that God is within every person and that when one feels directed by God, that guidance is more important than biblical teachings. Hicksite Quakers were often ridiculed—and worse—for these beliefs.

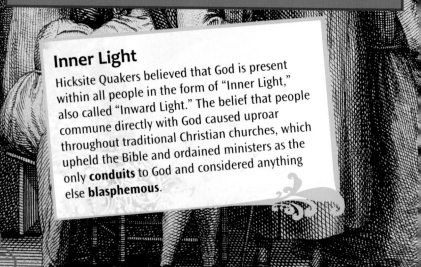

Inner Light

Hicksite Quakers believed that God is present within all people in the form of "Inner Light," also called "Inward Light." The belief that people commune directly with God caused uproar throughout traditional Christian churches, which upheld the Bible and ordained ministers as the only **conduits** to God and considered anything else **blasphemous**.

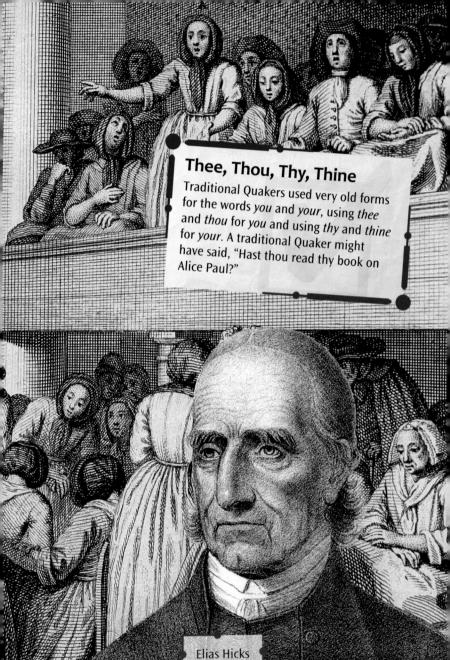

Thee, Thou, Thy, Thine

Traditional Quakers used very old forms for the words *you* and *your*, using *thee* and *thou* for *you* and using *thy* and *thine* for *your*. A traditional Quaker might have said, "Hast thou read thy book on Alice Paul?"

Elias Hicks

Quaker Influence

The Quaker faith and the community in which Paul was raised deeply shaped her life and convictions. Within her home and among the people of her sphere, gender equality was understood and honored. The minds and perspectives of women and men were respected. No value was placed on one gender over the other. The same was true for people of all races. Quakers see no **intrinsic** difference among people with differing racial identities. For Quakers, all rights are human rights, and they are **ordained** by God.

Always There

"When the Quakers were founded . . . one of their principles was and is equality of the sexes. So I never had any other idea . . . the principle was always there."—Alice Paul

Equally important to Quakers is the call to improve society whenever there is a problem. If a group of people is not treated fairly or given its natural rights, a Quaker must work to change that. For these reasons, the causes of women's rights and the **abolition** of slavery were very important to Quakers of Paul's time. Knowing this, it is understandable that the percentage of Quakers among suffragists and abolitionists was very high.

Simplicity

Quakers also support living a simple life. One might have wealth, but one should never be materialistic. The natural world is far more important than the material world. **Modesty** in dress, speech, and manner also supports a simple lifestyle.

the executive Committee of the Pennsylvania Anti-Slavery Society, 1851

Paul grew up in a community in which women and men were treated equally and offered equal opportunities. Upon learning that such equality wasn't practiced in the world outside her sphere, she became impassioned to change it. A fire was lit within her, and achieving equality became her driving force.

Because Quakers believe so fervently in equality, education for all is also one of their values. Paul always loved to learn. When she graduated from high school, it was only natural that she would attend college. Lucky for her that college was a big part of her family's life as well! Paul's grandfather, Judge William Parry, was cofounder of Swarthmore College. The Quaker-based college was one of the first coeducational schools, welcoming both men and women. Judge Parry had hopes that all students would benefit from such an education.

Female Graduates

During Paul's time, a high percentage of young men joined the work force in their high school years and didn't finish school. Because of this trend, in 1900 about 60 percent of all high school graduates were female. Despite that, only 19 percent of college graduates that same year were women.

About Swarthmore

Swarthmore College (below), founded in 1864, is a liberal arts college located south of Philadelphia, Pennsylvania. Although it began as a Quaker school, it lost its Quaker affiliation in the early twentieth century.

"Use Thy Gumption!"

In 1901, Paul began college at Swarthmore, where she had received a scholarship. All her siblings attended Swarthmore, but Paul was the only one to graduate. She earned a degree in biology.

At Swarthmore, a professor named Susan Cunningham influenced Paul. Cunningham encouraged all students to "use thy gumption" in everything they did. *Gumption* can be defined as conviction put into motion. It is spirit, resourcefulness, and a can-do attitude. Cunningham's words left a mark on Paul. She clearly used her gumption fully, not only in college but throughout her life.

Susan Cunningham: Breaking Barriers

Susan Cunningham was an important part of the early development of Swarthmore College. She helped to found the mathematics and astronomy departments. She developed and lived in Swarthmore's observatory, named the Cunningham Observatory. Cunningham was one of the first women to be a member of the American Mathematical Society. She was also an early member of the Astronomical Society of the Pacific. She was a popular figure at school and had an impact on countless students, including Paul. When she died in 1921, her funeral took place on campus. Her impact was so significant that even the state governor attended her funeral.

Also of significance to Paul's story is the fact that several of her professors were women. Few women were college professors at that time, but there were many female professors at Swarthmore. Just as in her childhood, Paul's world continued to include women in leadership roles that involved intellect and responsibilities normally reserved for men.

Paul at her Swarthmore College graduation in 1905

Here was evidence once again that a societal system of equality could and would be the right course everywhere, not just at Swarthmore.

College Cut Short

Paul's mother attended Swarthmore for three years but then had to leave the college. She got married, and married women were not allowed to attend college.

Always Learning

Paul's gumption took her far in her education. She had an active role in student government on campus. At graduation, she was designated "Ivy Poet" (an honor) and asked to write and recite an original poem. Paul also graduated as a member of Swarthmore's sorority.

To say that Paul had an interest in education is a huge understatement. Since few women in her day went further than high school, it is worthwhile to note that Paul continued her education beyond her first degree. She earned a certificate in social work from the New York School of Philanthropy. She also earned a master's degree in sociology from the University of Pennsylvania in 1907. She then spent three years studying social work at the University of London and the University of Birmingham. She returned to the University of Pennsylvania and in 1912 was awarded a doctorate in the same field. In 1922, she obtained another bachelor's degree, this time from the American University Washington College of Law. A master of law degree followed in 1927. A year later, she received her doctor of law degree!

While furthering her studies, Paul also continued her active sports life. In college, she played tennis, field hockey, and basketball.

Gumption? When talking about Alice Paul, it's hard to imagine a better word.

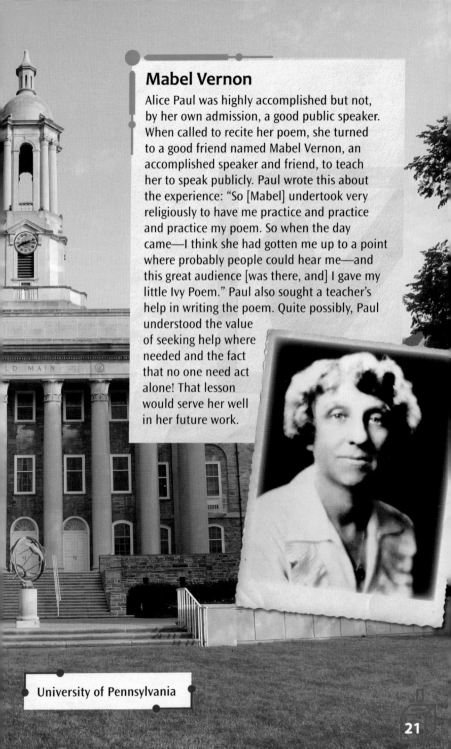

Mabel Vernon

Alice Paul was highly accomplished but not, by her own admission, a good public speaker. When called to recite her poem, she turned to a good friend named Mabel Vernon, an accomplished speaker and friend, to teach her to speak publicly. Paul wrote this about the experience: "So [Mabel] undertook very religiously to have me practice and practice and practice my poem. So when the day came—I think she had gotten me up to a point where probably people could hear me—and this great audience [was there, and] I gave my little Ivy Poem." Paul also sought a teacher's help in writing the poem. Quite possibly, Paul understood the value of seeking help where needed and the fact that no one need act alone! That lesson would serve her well in her future work.

University of Pennsylvania

Other Heroes on the Journey

Every hero's journey includes inspiring figures. Two of Alice Paul's key role models were Susan B. Anthony and Lucretia Mott. Both were Quakers who shared Paul's beliefs and **sensibilities**. They also preceded her efforts and helped pave the way for Paul's work.

Anthony was born into an abolitionist family in 1820. She lived her life working to end slavery, to reform education, to reform labor, to end alcohol abuse, and to grant women the right to vote. She worked tirelessly to generate change.

Susan B. Anthony

Money Talks

In 2016, it was decided that Anthony, Mott, Stanton, Sojourner Truth, and Paul would be pictured on the back of the U.S. $10 bill. These women, along with Harriet Tubman (on the $20 bill), are the first women to be shown on a U.S. bill since Martha Washington was featured on a $1 silver certificate in the 1880s and 1890s.

Mott was born in 1793. Like Anthony, she worked with her family to end slavery. She was also a lifetime advocate for women's rights. In 1848, she helped to organize the first women's rights convention at Seneca Falls. In 1850, she published *Discourse on Woman*, in which she argued for equal economic opportunities and voting. Mott also cofounded Swarthmore College. Both Anthony and Mott influenced others to join the women's rights effort.

Lucretia Mott

Elizabeth Cady Stanton

Stanton is often credited with igniting the U.S. women's rights movement. Her (and Mott's) Declaration of Sentiments was read at Seneca Falls. Through it, she motivated women and men to work for women's rights. But her interests went beyond just suffrage. Stanton advocated for women's right to income and property, to divorce, to have a say in family finances, to control how many children they had, and for their rights as parents. These were much wider concerns than many other activists pursued.

Elizabeth Cady Stanton

Seneca Falls

The first U.S. convention for women's rights took place in Seneca Falls, New York, in 1848. Organized by Lucretia Mott and Elizabeth Cady Stanton, it was a call to action, encouraging women to organize and petition for their rights. Twelve resolutions were passed at the convention. The ninth, "elective franchise" (a woman's right to vote in public elections), was hotly debated. The paraphrased resolutions are shown on the right.

The Seneca Falls convention was only the first of many women's rights conventions. Pictured here is Governor Frederick Gardner signing Missouri's ratification of the Nineteenth Amendment in 1920.

A President Declares . . .

In his second inaugural address, President Barack Obama declared, "We, the people, declare today that the most evident of truths—that all of us are created equal—is the star that guides us still; just as it guided our forebears through Seneca Falls, and Selma, and Stonewall." The three locations mark significant civil rights turning points.

Declaration of Sentiments

1. Laws should not be in conflict with women's happiness.

2. Laws should not prevent women from equal status with men.

3. Women are and should be recognized as men's equal.

4. Women should enlighten themselves about the laws.

5. Since men declare women morally superior, they should encourage and allow women to teach and speak at religious gatherings.

6. Men and women should be held to the same moral standards and suffer the same consequences for **transgressions**.

7. No one should accuse a woman of **impropriety** when she addresses a public gathering.

8. Women must break out of the confines applied to them over time.

9. Women should be granted the right to vote.

10. Human beings as a race are capable and responsible.

11. Having the same capabilities and consciousness, it is the right of every woman and man to teach and speak.

12. The success of women's rights depends on the efforts of women and men alike.

"Deeds Not Words"

Paul was in her early twenties in 1907 when she decided to pursue her education in England. Little did she know that her time there would radically change her life. She wanted to further her studies in social work, but over the next three years, she developed a passion for **militant** activism and earnestly joined the suffragist movement.

Although she'd always been committed to women's rights, a new passion was sparked in Paul when she met Christabel Pankhurst. When Paul first encountered her, Pankhurst was speaking to a crowd about suffrage. She was booed so loudly and relentlessly that she couldn't be heard at all and left the stage. Paul was disturbed by the exchange and sought out the speaker, soon learning all about Pankhurst and her mother and sister. They were radical suffragists who were changing the political landscape in England, and they'd had enough of petitions and waiting for change. They were ready for action—no matter what. "Deeds not words" was their motto, and they lived it every day.

Father Says

William Paul said of his daughter, "When there is a job to be done, I bank on Alice." Sadly, he died suddenly while his daughter was still a student at Swarthmore.

Christabel Pankhurst

Christabel Pankhurst (shown above) was beautiful and intelligent, commanding attention wherever she went. She chose to use her talents to support women's suffrage in England. Pankhurst was first noticed when she began shouting about women's rights at a political meeting. She was arrested for her outburst. It was the first of many arrests that would draw attention to her cause. While most suffragists worked for multiple social causes, Pankhurst focused solely on suffrage. She thought other causes would be managed once women could vote. Her tactics eventually succeeded when full suffrage for women came to England in 1928.

All in the Family

Christabel, along with her mother, Emmeline, and her sister, Sylvia, founded and ran the Women's Social and Political Union (WSPU) in 1903. The organization was based on bringing about change through action. After years of government promises without progress, the trio and the WSPU became militant. The group **heckled** opponents' speeches, broke windows, and disrupted meetings to bring attention to the cause. They harassed and even assaulted police officers. Their multiple arrests brought them public interest. In jail, they went on hunger strikes to protest and to draw even more attention to the cause. It was a harsh reality, but they knew a dead suffragist would generate public outrage—and they were willing to die for the cause. More and more people—especially women—joined their efforts thanks to the attention drawn by their drastic measures.

Christabel

Emmeline

Sylvia

Most Influential

TIME magazine named Emmeline one of the 100 most influential people of the twentieth century.

Emmeline Pankhurst
arrested in 1914

Emmeline Pankhurst

Emmeline's parents were politically active. Her husband, Richard Pankhurst, was a supporter of women's suffrage long before they met. Pankhurst herself came to the cause at the age of 14, and there was no turning back. She tried through the years to work within political parties to bring about social changes. But always, doors were slammed and little progress made. When she founded the WSPU after her husband's death, Pankhurst consciously chose to work outside political parties. Many people of the time (and today) ardently opposed the WSPU's militant tactics. Even so, no one can deny her **indelible** mark on history and role in achieving women's suffrage.

Ready for Battle

Alice Paul was inspired by the ferocious tenacity of the Pankhursts and the WSPU, and she eagerly joined their battle. Paul never saw herself as brave or as a public speaker, but she battled bravely and spoke often on the topic of rights for women. Working with the Pankhursts emboldened her. She disrupted lectures, obstructed meetings, and by her own account, broke 48 windows. With the Pankhursts and other suffragists, Paul was arrested many times, and like them, when arrested, she refused to eat. Jailers began to forcibly feed the striking suffragists by holding down their limbs and torsos, drawing back their heads, and forcing tubes down their throats or up their noses. They then sent liquid through the hoses so that the strikers received nutrients. According to the victims, the pain was excruciating, both physically and emotionally.

Thomas Jefferson once wrote, "Resistance to tyranny is obedience to God." Susan B. Anthony used his words as a mission. Paul read the words on a wall during one of her imprisonments, and she took them to heart. She would also take them and the WSPU motto, "deeds not words," with her when she returned to the United States to continue the fight.

Home from England

Returning to the United States in 1910, Paul said of her time in England: "The militant policy is bringing success . . . Women of England are now talking of the time when they will vote, instead of the time when their children would vote."

TORTURING WOMEN IN PRISON

Votes for Women

Published by THE NATIONAL WOMEN'S SOCIAL AND POLITICAL UNION ● Clements Inn, Strand W.C. ● Printed by DAVID ALLEN & SONS LE A11 FLEET ST ● 7512-23

VOTE AGAINST THE GOVERNMENT

THINK LINK

Activists throughout history have often fallen into two distinct camps: active resistance and peaceful resistance.

◎ What might be the benefits or concerns about each approach?

◎ What method of activism might be most effective in the long term? Why do you think so, and does history support your thinking?

◎ Is there a social cause for which you might consider activism?

"Iron Jawed Angels"

Back in the United States, Paul got down to work with renewed conviction. She wasn't alone in that. Other people—mainly women—grew increasingly passionate about the cause. Lucy Burns in particular shared Paul's vision. Burns and Paul became good friends and banded together to fight for suffrage. Newspapers would later dub the two and other militant suffragists "Iron Jawed Angels." Their fierce determination coupled with their presumed mild manner as women earned them the **moniker**.

Violence at the Parade

In 1912, Paul and Burns went to Washington, DC, to create support for the cause. They organized a huge parade. Ordinarily, a parade would not be especially newsworthy, but this parade would march down Pennsylvania Avenue right past the White House. And it would take place on President Woodrow Wilson's **inauguration** day, March 3, 1913.

The parade began peacefully but soon turned violent. A mob of men first hurled insults at the marchers and then physically attacked them while police officers watched. The marchers suffered the abuse, but they also made front-page news and brought suffrage to everyone's attention.

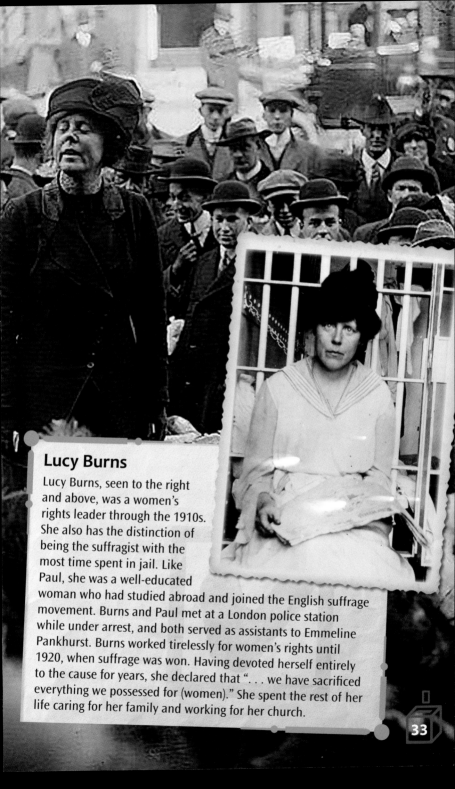

Lucy Burns

Lucy Burns, seen to the right and above, was a women's rights leader through the 1910s. She also has the distinction of being the suffragist with the most time spent in jail. Like Paul, she was a well-educated woman who had studied abroad and joined the English suffrage movement. Burns and Paul met at a London police station while under arrest, and both served as assistants to Emmeline Pankhurst. Burns worked tirelessly for women's rights until 1920, when suffrage was won. Having devoted herself entirely to the cause for years, she declared that ". . . we have sacrificed everything we possessed for (women)." She spent the rest of her life caring for her family and working for her church.

National Women's Party

In 1912, Paul and Burns were named co-chairs of a congressional committee working for the National American Woman Suffrage Association (NAWSA). The committee was formed to **lobby** for a suffrage amendment to the U.S. Constitution. Paul was convinced that an amendment was the most important next step in the fight.

NAWSA's president, Carrie Chapman Catt, was also an active suffragist. She disagreed with Paul. Her interest was in working state by state to effect change. Catt and NAWSA also wanted to work closely with **Democrats**, believing that allying with that party would help to generate change. NAWSA endorsed President Wilson, a Democrat.

"New World Order"

"There will never be a new world order until women are a part of it."—Alice Paul

Paul strongly disagreed. She believed that every political figure should be held responsible for change and be made accountable until an amendment was **ratified**.

Paul and Catt could not come to an agreement. Finally, in 1916, Paul and Burns formed a party called the National Women's Party (NWP). Its tactics and interests were very much like those of England's WSPU, and it strove to keep suffrage in the public eye.

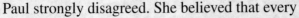

35

STOP! THINK...

Suffragists such as Paul used everything available to them to sway public opinion and get the attention of lawmakers. This included the use of propaganda posters such as the one above, which was in support of the WSPU.

- ◎ What central message is the poster trying to convey?
- ◎ Is the poster effectively persuasive?
- ◎ How might a propaganda poster work against a group's message?

"Silent Sentinels"

The NWP was on a mission. The group wanted to keep the demand for an amendment front and center in the nation's mind and also in the president's. They arranged for women called "Silent Sentinels" to stand outside the White House with banners protesting and **defaming** the president. They said nothing, but their haunting presence and **incendiary** banners spoke volumes.

President Wilson tolerated the Sentinels until the United States was drawn into World War I. He and many others believed that the suffragists should step down during the war so that all energies could be focused on war efforts. But Paul and others like her believed that the time was more appropriate than ever to battle for the vote. In fact, Paul believed that until the United States demonstrated an inclusive democracy for all, fighting for democracy elsewhere in the world was wrong.

Once the war started, onetime hecklers and harassers of the Sentinels became fully abusive. The women were frequently arrested under **fabricated** criminal charges. In jail, the suffragists were threatened and abused. Some were sent to insane asylums. As women, they had few rights and little recourse to protect and defend themselves.

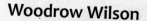

Woodrow Wilson

A former New Jersey governor, Wilson served as president of the United States from 1913 to 1921. Wilson was known for his support of **progressive** causes. He advocated for peace and worked to keep the country out of the war. He even won the Nobel Peace Prize in 1919. But he also actively opposed women's right to vote until his hand was forced just after the war, which ended in 1918. Because of his resistance, suffragists labeled him Kaiser Wilson, after the despised Kaiser of Germany.

PRESIDENT WILSON IS DECEIVING THE WORLD
WHEN HE APPEARS AS THE PROPHET OF DEMOCRACY
PRESIDENT WILSON HAS OPPOSED THOSE WHO
DEMAND DEMOCRACY FOR THIS COUNTRY
HE IS RESPONSIBLE FOR THE DISFRANCHISEMENT
OF MILLIONS OF AMERICANS
WE IN AMERICA KNOW THIS
THE WORLD WILL FIND HIM OUT.

"Night of Terror"

The frequency and duration of the suffragists' arrests escalated. Most people said their efforts during wartime were unpatriotic, but Paul and her colleagues would not relent and chose to fight even harder.

In November 1917, 33 protesters and members of the NWP were locked in prison, including Paul and Burns. Many had been arrested and given prison time for the charge of obstructing traffic. In prison, the women were regularly beaten and abused, given spoiled food, and locked away in "punishment cells." The sick were denied medical care, and rats ran wild at their feet. But on the "Night of Terror," the abuse was even more devastating. The guards and the prison superintendent of the Occoquan Workhouse in Virginia tortured the women, painfully force-fed them, and terrorized them. At least one was hung by shackles on her wrists. No one came to their aid.

Approximately two weeks after they went to prison, the women finally received a hearing. In it, the judge found that they were illegally arrested and held without cause. They were all released; however, no mention was made of the "Night of Terror," and no charges were ever brought against the jailers.

A Change of Tune

Early in 1918, President Wilson declared that it was in the interest of the war effort to support women's suffrage.

Suffragists protest on the steps of the U.S. Capitol building in 1917.

Nineteenth Amendment

Women's suffrage came to pass when the Nineteenth Amendment to the Constitution was ratified on August 18, 1920, and then passed into law on August 26. Through the efforts of Anthony, Mott, Stanton, Paul, and other leaders, all women in the United States finally had the right to vote and participate in elections. It was 72 years from the first convention in Seneca Falls. It was 50 years since the Fifteenth Amendment was passed. But success was at hand, at long last. The heart of the Nineteenth Amendment reads as follows:

The right of citizens of the United States to vote shall not be denied or abridged by the United States or by any State on account of sex.

August 26 is now celebrated each year as Women's Equality Day.

Tennessee for the Win

The U.S. House and Senate passed the amendment in 1919. Three-fourths of the states then needed to ratify it. The decision rested with Tennessee—more specifically, with Harry Burn, a young assemblyman. He wanted to vote against the resolution but changed his mind after receiving a message from his mother. She asked him to support it—and he did, breaking the tie and officially ratifying the amendment.

"Ordinary Equality"

"I never doubted that equal rights was the right direction. Most reforms, most problems are complicated. But to me there is nothing complicated about ordinary equality."

—*Alice Paul, 1972*

Passage of the Nineteenth Amendment was an enormous, hard-won victory, but for Paul, it was not the end. Suffrage was important, but there was so much more to be done. Paul's ultimate goal was equal rights under the law in all things. In 1923, she drafted the "Lucretia Mott Amendment," also known as the Equal Rights Amendment (ERA). It stated, "Men and women shall have equal rights throughout the United States and every place subject to its jurisdiction."

The ERA was brought before Congress every year from 1923 through 1972, and in the last year, it finally passed and was sent to the states to ratify. There was a seven-year deadline (later changed to 10 years) for ratification by three-fourths of the states. In 1982, the ERA had failed by three states.

Alice Paul died on July 9, 1977. She never married or had children. She dedicated the entirety of her life to women's rights. The convictions of her youth were the convictions of her lifetime. She lived her life as one of the greatest activists, social-justice advocates, and civil rights leaders of all time.

World Woman's Party (WWP)

In 1938, Paul started the WWP in Geneva, Switzerland. Its purpose was to bring rights to women throughout the world.

Alice Paul Amendment

In 1943, the ERA was rewritten and named after its fiercest advocate and given a new nickname—the "Alice Paul Amendment."

Alice Paul

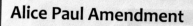

Glossary

abolition—the act of officially ending slavery

blasphemous—perceived as highly disrespectful to God

clergy—the leaders of a Christian religion who lead church services and ceremonies

conduits—religious leaders who can receive and deliver divine messages

conviction—the feeling of being certain in your beliefs

crucial—essential

defaming—harming the name or character of a person, usually through false words

Democrats—members of one of the major political parties in the United States

dissent—public disagreement

fabricated—made up

Friends—members of the Christian group, formally known as the Religious Society of Friends, that practices pacifism and has no clergy

fundamental—basic

heckled—insulted

ideology—belief system

impropriety—rude behavior

inauguration—starting day

incendiary—causing anger

indelible—unable to be forgotten

intrinsic—part of the nature of something

lobby—work together in a large, organized group to influence government

means—money or resources

militant—demonstrating organized, forceful methods to achieve a goal

modesty—sexually reserved behavior

moniker—nickname

ordained—made an official religious leader; established by decree

pacifism—the belief in not using violence to resolve conflicts

progressive—in favor of change, improvement, or reform

Quakers—nickname for members of the Religious Society of Friends

ratified—made a document official, usually through a voting process

resolute—determined

sensibilities—feelings, especially in response to things that are seen, heard, or experienced

suffrage—the right to vote and participate in politics

tenacity—strong determination

transgressions—violations of the law or moral guidelines

undaunted—determined to keep going no matter the obstacles

Index

Check It Out!

Books

Baker, Jean H. 2006. *Sisters: The Lives of America's Suffragists*. Hill and Wang.

Herweck, Dona. 2012. *Susan B. Anthony*. Teacher Created Materials.

Kamma, Anne. 2008. *If You Lived When Women Won Their Rights*. Scholastic.

Robbins, Dean. 2016. *Miss Paul and the President: The Creative Campaign for Women's Right to Vote*. Knopf Books for Young Readers.

Videos

Gavron, Sarah. 2015. *Suffragette*. Ruby Films.

Von Garnier, Katja. 2004. *Iron Jawed Angels*. Home Box Office.

Wattenberg, Ben J. 2000. *The First Measured Century: The Other Way of Looking at American History*. PBS Home Video.

Websites

Alice Paul Institute. *Who Was Alice Paul*. http://www.alicepaul.org/who-was-alice-paul/.

A&E. *History: Alice Paul*. http://www.history.com/topics/womens-history/alice-paul.

Try It!

During the suffrage movement, propaganda posters and political comics were used against and in support of women's rights. Imagine you are a columnist for your local newspaper. You are tasked with the job of creating two political cartoons or two propaganda posters.

◎ Think about something you are passionate about. What is a cause that you hold dear to your heart? Do you want to stop someone or a group of people from doing something? Do you want to change the way things are run? Do you feel a policy could be executed more efficiently? Make a list of the causes you come up with.

◎ Look over your list. As a journalist, you must be impartial. Pick an argument that you can create two posters or political cartoons for—one that supports the cause and one that is against the cause.

◎ Now that you have made a selection, create a list of arguments for each side of the cause.

◎ Decide whether making political cartoons or propaganda posters would be the best way to get each of your points across. This may require researching historical examples. Think about what makes a strong and persuasive poster. What are some techniques that political cartoonists use to get their points across?

◎ Create a draft of your posters or political cartoons. Be sure to include words, symbols, phrases, and arguments that each side would likely make.

◎ Have a friend look over your work and add suggestions for changes that could make your work stronger and/or clearer.

◎ Finalize your posters or cartoons.

About the Author

Dona Herweck Rice vividly remembers the push for the ratification of the Equal Rights Amendment and how, even as a young girl, she worked for its passage. Her personal heroes include Alice Paul and all leaders in the fight for women's rights, and she will be forever grateful for their tireless work and sacrifices. She knows that these wonderful women who've gone before her are a big reason why she can do the work she loves today, which is writing books like this one. She has written hundreds of books for children and educators and, even as she writes these words, she eagerly looks forward to the next topic!